Strategy Implementation and Control Analysis in Business

Hiriyappa. B, Ph.D.

Contents

Chapter 1. Interrelationships Between Strategy Formulation and Implementation

Chapter 2. Issues in Strategy Implementation

Chapter 3. Organisation and Strategy Implementation

Chapter 4. Organization Structure and Organisational Design

Chapter 5. Types of Organizational Structure

Chapter 6. Integration and Integrating Mechanisms

Chapter 7. The Value Chain

Chapter 8 Concept of Corporate Culture

Chapter 9. Strategic Leadership

Chapter 10. Strategic Control Systems

CHAPTER 1
INTERRELATIONSHIPS BETWEEN STRATEGY FORMULATION AND IMPLEMENTATION

"Winning companies know how to do their work better".
Michael Hammer and James Champy

"A management truism says structure follows strategy. However, this truism is often ignored. Too many organizations attempt to carry out a new strategy with an old Structure".
Dale McConkey

"Weak leadership can wreck the soundest strategy; forceful execution of even a poor plan can often bring victory".
By – Sun zi

"An organization's capacity to execute its strategy depends on its "hard" infrastructure - Its organizational structure and systems

and on its "soft" infrastructure its culture and norms".
By – Amar Bhide

"The biggest levers you've got to change a company are strategy, structure, and culture. If I could pick two, I'd pick strategy".
By- Wayne Leonard, CEO, Entergy

"The ideal organizational structure is a place where ideas filter up as well as down, where the merit of ideas carries more weight than their source, and where participation and shared objectives are valued more than executive order".
Edson Spencer

"Leader lives in the field with his troops".
H – Ross Perot

"Weak leadership can wreck the soundest strategy; forceful execution of even a poor plan can often bring victory".
Sun Zi

INTRODUCTION

In this book, we shall discuss the concept of strategy formulation, to know the relationships between strategy formulation and implementation of the strategy, to study different issues in strategy formulation. Design the organization structure for strategy formulation and implementation and control in terms of functional structure, divisional structure, strategic business units, matrix structure and network structure. Strategy implementation and control in strategic business units and core competencies are related to value chain analysis, identifying the core competencies and manages it links with business. It also involves leadership which helpful for strategic implementation. While implementation of strategy in an organization would be building a strategy which is supporting corporate culture for proper implementation and control. Finally, strategic management is a continuous process in firms which decides what strategies will be required by the enterprise. In this case, there must be the translation of strategic thought into strategic action in the enterprise and its process. Proper translation requires the support of all managers and employees of the business: it is the basic essential to the enterprise. Improper implementation of the strategy, it affects to the entire organization. It affects all the functional and divisional areas of a business.

INTERRELATIONSHIPS BETWEEN STRATEGY FORMULATION AND IMPLEMENTATION

Strategy execution deals with the managerial exercise and it involves to the supervision of organization for ongoing strategy formulation and execution in an enterprise for survival, growth, and development in an organization.

Strategy execution will be making work, it can be improving the core competencies are implemented and showing measurable progress towards the achievement of the targets results.

It is concerned with the translation a decision which converts into action that is pre purposeful and makes the proper decision itself.

Strategy implementation should be acceptable and to know the feasibility of the performance in an organization.

It involves the allocation of resources to the new course of action which will be undertaken by a company.

It designs the organization structure and its activities for effective handling in an organization.

BASIC ELEMENTS OF STRATEGIC MANAGEMENT

Basic elements of strategic management involve to strategy formulation, implementation, and control of strategy in the enterprise or organization or company

Basic elements of strategic management are classified into three steps

Step one is to Strategic analysis; it consists of the environment, expectations and purposes and resources competencies and capability.

Step second is to strategic choice; it principally the combination of bases of strategic choice, strategic options and strategic evaluation and selection.

The third step is to strategic implementation: it composes of organization structure and design, resource allocation and control, managing strategic change.

STRATEGY FORMULATION AND IMPLEMENTATION MATRIX

There are so many differences between strategy formulation and implementation process. So many managers in enterprises fail to make distinguish between strategy formulation and implementation. Strategy formulation requires special skills and also strategy implementation also requires very different skills compare to strategy formulation. An organization is successful due to its credit goes to sound strategy formulation and implementation of strategy and control tool of strategy. In several cases, strategy formulation and implementation is the failure due to lack knowledge, skills, and resources in the project.

Matrix clearly identified the distinction between sound / flawed strategy formulation and excellent/weak strategy implementation. It identified with the Square A, B, C, D'.

Square A refers to the situation where a company seems to formulate a very competitive strategy, but it is showing difficulties, in the case of implementation it successfully. It happens due to the lack of experience, the lack of resources, missing leadership and so on. In these situations, the company will be aiming at moving from A to B. In this case, project managers and a team will be facing some difficulties in implementation of projects.

Square B refers to the ideal situation where a company has been succeeded in designing a sound and competitive strategy and it has been successfully implemented in the enterprise.

Square C refers to the reserved for companies, but hasn't succeeded in coming up with a sound strategy formulation and in addition, are bad at implementing their flawing strategic model. In this case, it is ready to go success when it goes through the business model redesign and implementation or execution with a readjustment in projects.

Square D refers to the situation where the strategy formulation is flawed; in this case, a company is showing excellent implementation skills. It finds itself in square D and the first thing is to redesign their strategy before readjusting their implementation or execution skills in projects.

Principal Combinations of Efficiency and Effectiveness Focus Strategy in Organization.

Studying before Efficiency and Effectiveness we shall know about the reasons for failure, such as a lack of strategic direction, guidance, suggestions, and recommendations, lack of resources. These are created the tendency to look inwards at times of stress. And for management to devote their attention to cost cutting and to shedding unprofitable divisions in business units in an organization.

Efficiency is the introspective to attain goals which achieved by each level employee in the organization in this way focus on efficiency and effectiveness organization.

Efficiency and effectiveness is core responsibilities of the strategic managers, top management will be having the primary responsibilities towards the efficiency and effectiveness to highlight the main orientation of the organization.

Effectiveness highlights the links between the organization and the environment.

Highlights operational management efficiency and inefficiency and also strategic management effective and ineffective situations in an organization for thriving, die slowly, survive and die quickly circumstances in this way achieved with an efficient output and input ratio.

Cell 1 refers to thrive in an organization, it finds and refers to well-placed and it can be achieved what it aspires to achieve with an efficient output or input ratio.

Cell 2 refers die slowly, it is doomed, unless it can establish some strategic direction towards the efficient output or input ratio.

Cell 3 refers to survive, it is possible when increased the efficiency and effectiveness towards the output and input ratio in an organization.

Cell 4 refers to Die quickly and it is doomed, in this situation organization take the quick strategic decision.

Results of Efficiency and Effectiveness

Major results of efficiency and effectiveness in an enterprise as outlined:

It is in the form of the dividend to shareholders.

Wages to employees.
Continued business with suppliers of goods and services.

Satisfaction on the part of customers and consumers.

Legal requirement fulfillment from the point view of government.

Responsible behavior towards society and environment from the perspective of pressure groups in the society.

CONTRAST BETWEEN STRATEGY FORMULATION AND IMPLEMENTATION

The major contrast between strategy formulation and implementation are outlined:

Strategy Formulation is positioned forces before the action, whereas Strategy implementation is managing forces during the course of action.

Strategy Formulation is focused on effectiveness but Strategy implementation is focused on efficiency.

Strategy Formulation is primarily an intellectual process Whereas Strategy implementation is primarily and operational process.

Strategy Formulation is required good intuitive and analytical skills whereas, Strategy implementation is required special motivation and leadership skills.

Strategy Formulation requires coordination among a few individuals in the project, whereas Strategy implementation requires a combination among many individuals in a project.

Strategy Formulation is primarily an entrepreneurial activity that based on strategic decisions making process, but Strategy implementation is mainly an administrative task based on strategic as well as operational decision making.

Strategic tools and concepts are very important for the formulation of strategy which is not distinguished greatly for small, large, for-profit, or nonprofit organizations. Therefore, strategy formulation varies significantly among different types and sizes of organizations. Meanwhile, implementation strategies required in the following cases:

Altering sales territories
Adding new departments

Closing facilities

Hiring new employees

Changing of organization pricing policy and its strategy

Develop financial budgets

Develop new employee's benefits

Establishing cost control procedures

Changing Advertising Strategies

Building New Facilities

Training New Employees

Transferring The Managers Among the Divisions

Building A Better Management Information System

Above mentioned activities are differently greatly among the manufacturing, services, and government owned organizations.

STRATEGIC MANAGEMENT LINKAGES

Strategic management linkages are very important for the purpose of orderly study in an organization. In the real scenario of strategic formulation and implementation, processes are interlinked with each other. There are two types of linkages exist between the strategy formulation and implementation phase are

Forward Linkages and Backward Linkages.

Forward Linkages

It deals with the impact of the formulation on implementation of strategies in the enterprise.

There are different elements are required for strategy formulation that starting with the mission and vision setting through environmental and organizational appraisal, strategic alternatives and choice of the strategic plan which determine and applicable to an organization.

It involves the formulation of new strategies or reformulation of existing strategies, which may change and have to be effected within the organization.

For example, when an organization structure has undergone change, this time, formulation of new strategies are crucial, otherwise undergone reformulation of existing strategies and try to make changes for dramatic improvement in organizational structure for implementation of the strategy.

Backward Linkages

It concerned with the impact in terms of opposite directions in an organization. i.e., Implementation is determined by the formulation of strategies. In this scenario, the formulation process is also affected by factors which are relating to implementation.

It deals with strategic choice, in this circumstance, strategist remembers the past strategic actions and process which determine and choose the best choice strategy.

Strategist tends to adopted past strategies which already implemented in an organization. In this case, strategist takes help from implemented strategy and design the appropriate strategies as per meet present requirement of the organization along with added special features in these strategies. These type incremental changes helpful to an organization for very long time survival in the market.

CHAPTER 2
ISSUES IN STRATEGY IMPLEMENTATION

INTRODUCTION

There are so many issues are essential for implementation of the project in real time scenario. Strategist task is very important to identify the different issues in different projects. These issues are based on strategist own experience, skills, knowledge, attitudes and abilities. The implement task helps to strategist to put their skills, knowledge, attitudes and abilities to test in terms of proper allocations of resources, design structures, formulate functional policies and take into consideration of leadership styles and how to deal with various issues in organization as listed below:

It involves the strategic planning that set by the organization, it proposes and put into action through the implementation of the project.

Always strategies should lead to plans. For example, a company has been formulated grand strategies, which leads to modernization or organization plan that requires to meet goals, policies, procedures, rules, and steps to be taken in putting a plan into action for survival, growth, development.

Project programmes which lead to the formulation of projects. A project programme is a highly specific program, it determines the time schedule and cost involved in the project. For this purpose, strategist to make a budget for allocations of resources. Research and Development programmes may consist of several projects which is intentioned to achieve specific and limited objective, these are required to allocations of funds, and has also set the time schedule to finish projects.

Projects have to require adequate infrastructure facilities which meet in day to day operations in an organization. It involves may be setting up new or additional infrastructure facilities, it requires new installation of newer systems, and several other activities that are needed for the implementation of strategies in business.

Implementation of strategies is not constraints to the formulation of plans, programmes and projects resource is essential to all types of project. Each project properly designed the organization structure, system requirements, planning tools, and strategic role of strategist to make plans and work as per planned and organized manner in projects.

ISSUES IN PROJECTS IMPLEMENTATION

Major issues which are relating to projects implementation as outlined in a sequential manner:
- Project implementation
- Procedural implementation
- Resource Allocation
- Structural implementation
- Functional implementation
- Behavioral implementation

These are the issues in project implementation are noted in the sequence, it does not mean that each of the issues in project implementation activities is necessarily performed one after another. Project implementation process activities can be performed simultaneously, in several cases, certain other activities will be repeated over time, in some cases, these activities are performed only once.

STRATEGIC RESPONSIBILITIES TOWARDS PROJECT IMPLEMENTATION

Strategic responsibilities are playing vital role in the formulation of strategy and implementation of projects in an organization.

For strategy formulation and implementation strategy requires a shift in responsibilities from the divisional and functional strategic managers in an organization.

Each project must be clearly defined the strategic role of divisional managers and functional managers in an organization.

Improper design organization responsibilities have to create so many problems in project formulation and implementation.

Decisions should be considered by middle and lower levels in projects in organizations, it is helpful to build good coordination and middle and lower level employees have participated in the strategic decision process.

Managers and employees are motivated by themselves and perceived their self-interest along with organization interest otherwise both are coinciding in projects.

Divisional and functional managers are involved in the formulation of strategy activities in an organization and provide equal importance to all categories of employees involved as possible in strategy formulation activities in an organization.

CENTRAL MANAGEMENT ISSUES IN STRATEGY IMPLEMENTATION

Central management issues in strategy implementation are listed below:

Change only for improvement of business process.

Cultural diversity and adoption and operation of an organization.

Development of support culture strategy in an organization.

Devising policies in an organization.

Downsizing an organization, it is doing when it is necessary for the organization.

Effective development of human resource role in an organization

Establishing annual objectives.

Mangers act as a strategic role in an organization.

Proper allocation of available resource

Ready for altering an existing organizational structure.

Restructuring and reengineering.

Revising rewarding and incentives policies in an organization.

Strategic mangers changes should direct to firm to move towards new directions for achievement, survival, growth and over all development of an organization in short-term and long-term in business.

MANGERS AND EMPLOYEES PARTICIPATION IN PROJECT IMPLEMENTATION

Managers and employees can be participated early and directly involved in strategy formulation and implementation decisions throughout an organization.

They are participating in for a strategy implementation in this way buildup project design for implementation in an organization.

Managers, employees and strategist's genuine commitment is very important to finish the implementation process in an organization.

These personnel require a powerful motivate themselves and others in an organization.

These personnel are busy towards strategy formulation and implementation activities in an organization.

They try to learn new things and the cop with the modern business environment.

Strategist and employees should understand clearly the mission and vision of the organization and clearly communicated throughout an organization.

These personnel are discussing the following things:

Who are major competitors?

What are the major accomplishments?

What are the products and services offered to customers?

What are the plans?

What is the action plan?

What is the performance of an organization?

What are the major external opportunities?

What are the internal opportunities?

What is authority and responsibilities?

What is role in the project?

What is the cost of the project?

What is the time schedule of the Project?

What are the hurdles in projects?

What are hierarchy position and its influence to an organization?

CHAPTER 3
ORGANISATION AND STRATEGY IMPLEMENTATION

NATURE OF STRATEGIC CHANGE MANAGEMENT

To change is to move from the present to the future, from known information to relatively unknown information. Therefore, change can be defined as "to make or become different, give or begin to have a different form". For example, post war recovery of Iraq and Afganstan. Change also refers to dissatisfaction with the old values, beliefs and systems and hence adapts to new values, beliefs and systems. The deficiency also reflects the inability of the system to respond to environmental changes. Change signifies a qualitatively different way of perceiving, thinking and behaving to make improvements over the past and present trends of the business management.

Change line context of an organization can be termed as a process of bringing about relatively enduring alteration in the present status of an organization or its components or interrelationships among the components and their differentiated and integrated functions in totally or partially. Therefore, changes in organization have attained greater adaptability and viability with reference to the current and emerging environmental developments in the world.

Strategic change in the organization has signified alteration in the objectives, goals and strategies, procedures for converting input into outputs, its specified features, structures and human resource. Changes in these are, however, inter-related in the organization. Thus, it may include product and process restructuring, mergers and alliances, diversification and installing new systems. It may also mean change in attitudes and skills of organizational human resource, tasks and technology of the enterprise, alteration in customs responsive, norms and culture. These changes are essential and needed for business enterprise.

In view of its pervasive nature, change at anyone level is interrelated with changes at other levels of the enterprise. Therefore, it is essential for the management to assess organization with wide implications of any change is going to be affected. Further, these changes need to be reviewed on a continuous basis to cope with ever changing environmental developments in business enterprise.

All changes are happening either in reaction to it as driving forces or a proactive. Changes have been planned and initiated by an organization. Therefore, reactive change happens in response to an event or series of events relating to business. The failure of existing process or system is a powerful mode for change in business. Reactive change being unplanned is hardly welcomed because it usually results in poorly coordinated, inefficient management. It plays havoc with virtually any strategic plan. Proactive changes take place when an organization's managers have concluded that a change would be beneficial to business. Proactive change is more orderly, more efficient because it is planned, structured and organized.

A change in an organization is directed at the micro level. It focused on units /subunits /components within an organization and brought in gradually are incremental changes. It is beneficial to an organization and built new skills and beliefs in the organization. These changes are efficient and acceptable by an organization. Many argue that such incremental development can be proactively managed; organization will keep in touch with the environment development and anticipate needs for change. This can be achieved through the process of changing of the current operating business system. Others argue that while it is not always possible to anticipate the need for major strategic changes, therefore, organizations react to external competitive or environmental pressures. Corporate managers may not perceive the need for major changes. In addition, adapt the existing paradigms and extent ways of operations.

However, incremental time changes may not be beneficial to the organization. Because such changes are based on the condition by the existing paradigms and routines of the organization even when the environmental developments are so cataclysmic and forceful systems and procedures in terms of basic assumptions, culture, technology etc. of the organization. These changes are transformational in character. Therefore, transformational change refers to changes that cannot be handled within the existing paradigms and organizational change; it may be taken from the granted assumptions. Transformational change may also take from as a result of either reactive or proactive process. If strategic drift has occurred or if external stakeholders are not happy due to the adequacy of current objective and strategy to meet the external threat of the organization. In this situation, management may be in a forced transformational position. Likewise, if other changes happened in the organizational environment are very powerful to the business issues. The organization is constrained to go for transformation change. Where managers anticipate the need for transformational change, meanwhile they get time to act upon the desired change.

Change can be distinguished on the basis of the degree of innovation is previously done in the organization. Innovation has brought changes in the organization. Innovation is different from change. Innovation occurs when an organization is the first time or early user of an innovative idea among its set of similar organizations in the business. Change brings a modification of the operating system of organization. Since innovation provides more excitement in change management. It is highly organized and systematic approach. It is exclusively concerned with reasoning what triggers change in the existing operating system and how affect the change in business. The management process programme is proactive, it monitors the continuously environmental developments for identifying the emerging opportunities and find out the suitable existing policies, strategies and programmes to exploit of these opportunities.

Another distinguishing characteristic of change management programme, it is the engagement of the entire organization in the change process because people have always been and will remain important. Organization wide involvement of organizational people is the crux of change management

IMPLEMENTING STRATEGIC CHANGE: STEPS IN THE CHANGING PROCESS

The management of strategic change involves serious steps that managers must follow if the change process is to be succeeding. The major important steps are listed below:

Determining the need for change
Determining the obstacles to change
Implementing change
Evaluating change
Determining the need for change

Determining the need for change

According to Sunbeam's turnaround suggests, the first step in the change process involves determining the need for change, analyzing the organization current position and determining the ideal future state that strategic managers would like it to attain, we are conducting a swot analysis, first we examine strengths and weakness. Once identified strength, weakness then determines the change of the management.

Determining Obstacles to Changes

The second step in the change processes is determining the obstacles to change. The Strategist must analyse the factors such as corporate, divisional, functional and individual. These factors are causing organizational inertia and preventing the company from reaching its ideal future state at the corporate level strategy seemingly trivial ways may significantly affect company's behavior some corporate culture is easier to change than others.

Implementing Change

Implementing change stage is introducing and managing changes

raises several questions generally, a company can take two main approaches to change. They are listed below:
   Top down change
   Bottom up change

In the case of Top down change approach CEO implements changes in the organization. Bottom up change approach, in the case low level management response to top level made changes in the organizational decision-making.

Evaluating Change
This is the last step in the changes process. It is to evaluate the effects of the changes in strategy and structure on organization performance. It is more difficult, however, to assess the effects of changes in structure on company performance.

CHAPTER 4
ORGANIZATION STRUCTURE AND ORGANISATIONAL DESIGN

WHAT IS A STRUCTURE?

Structure is the basic and simple concept: it is the division of task for efficiency and clarity of purpose in organization. It is coordination between the interdependent functional parts of the organization to ensure organizational effectiveness. Organization structure balances are in the need for specialization with the need for integration. It is provided for decentralizing and centralizing that consistent with the organizational and control needs of the strategy.

REASONS FOR ORGANIZATION STRUCTURE

There are two reasons for organization structure due to changes in strategy as listed below:

Organization structure largely explains how objectives and policies will be established.

Why changes in strategy often require changes in the structures that organization structure explains how resources will be allocated in an organization.

Chandler's Strategy - Structure Relationship

Chandler's strategy structure is very important to design the strategy and structure in the organization. It is designed in a different organization structure and its shows the relationship between strategy and organization structure to evaluate the different changes in strategy in different organizational structure.

Chandler's strategy - structure relationship found a particular structure sequence to be often repeated as organizations grow and change strategy overtime. It clearly highlights the there is no one optimal organization design or structure for giving a strategy or type of organization.

Chandler's Strategy Structure Relationship

An organization frame new strategy. It creates new administrative problems and organizational performance declines. At this time an organization has to establish new structure, it helps to an organization to improve its performance.

When we shall implement the new strategy, it creates so many administrative problems are emerging in terms of internal and external forces in the environment. When an organization neglects its problems and mission and objects that time organizational performance is declining due to improper design of strategy – structure relationship. Strategist takes care and design proper organizational structure and suitable strategy structure relationship; it will be brought to a new organizational structure should be established in the enterprise. Well defined strategy and structure relationship creates very good work environment in this way organizational performance is improved in the business.

WHAT IS ORGANISATIONAL DESIGN?

Designing an organization's structure is the task of management who have the responsibility of designing, implementing and achieving the organization's mission. This is accomplished by dividing the work of the organization and then coordinating the various responsibilities. It defines how the organization's goals will be reached and how the work will be done. This is a complex task, to assemble or alter a system. Designing an organization's frame work involves issues like complexity, formalization, centralization and determines what level of each will be required. It considers advance technology and environment to determine the appropriate structure to achieve organizational strategy.

Organizational structure is the company's formal configuration; it describes the roles, procedures, governance mechanisms, authority, and decision making process, responsivity, delegation of authority. It influences to an organization and its age and size and nature of businesses.

These factors are influenced to strategist to form a new strategy and implement strategy in functional division. It acts as a design a strategic framework which applies to functional division in an organization.

Organization structure is very essential to form a strategy, implement strategy and control strategy in an organization. Stable organization structure is required by the companies to discharge their day to day tasks in an organization to finish task completely. Effective strategic leaders should seek to develop an organization structure and to provide a control tool to strategist to manage the functions in an organization.

CHAPTER 5
TYPES OF ORGANIZATIONAL STRUCTURE

VERTICAL DIFFERENTIATION

Vertical differentiation is an important element of an organizational structure. It is to specify the reporting relationships that link people, tasks and functions at all levels of a company or organization. It means that management chooses the appropriate number of hierarchical levels and the correct span of control for implementing a company's strategy effectively. The organizational hierarchy establishes to span of control i.e. authority flows the top to bottom. The basic choice is a flat structure or tall structure.

Problems with Tall Hierarchies

Problems with Tall Hierarchies are as listed below:

Coordination problems in organization

Motivational problems in organization

Information problems in organization

Number of middle managers in organization

Coordination Problems in organization

The Organization consists of different variety employees perform their activities for accomplishment of goals. In this case employees are not coordinated to perform their duties effectively and efficiently. Therefore, it arises in the organization due to inadequate communication of top level, middle level and low level employees in an organization.

Motivational Problems in Organization

Organizational hierarchy is essential to need for motivational aspects to motivate of employees who are performing their duties in organization. Praises, recognize and additional improvement of facilities and perk to employees these are the motives for employees in an organization. Some times top management motivates their employees in terms of punishment. It is also one of the major problems of the organization structure.

Information Problems
Management hierarchy wants to new information from the customers, bankers, shareholders, debt holder, financial institution, and internal human resource of the organization. It has delay to provide to adequate information. Thus, it is one of the problems of the hierarchy structure.

Number of Middle management
Organization is a big, which appointed more middle level managers to manage and control the organization. Therefore, it is expensive for an organization. This factor also one of the unhealthy factors of the organization structure.

Vertical differentiation
It further classified into two broad categories. They are as follows:
Centralization
Decentralization

Centralization

Authority centralizes when mangers at the top levels of the organizational hierarchy retains the authority to make the most important decisions. Now days, the centralization of organizational structure is not important to formulation, implementation and monitor and controlling of the objectives of an organization.

Decentralization

When the authority is decentralized, it is delegated to divisions, functional departments and managers at lower levels in the organization. Some important strategic factors are related to the formulation, implementation and monitor and controlling the major objectives of an organization.

Strategic mangers delegate operational decision making responsibility to middle managers. Therefore, it reduces information overload to strategic managers in organization. In addition, strategic managers can spend more time on strategic decision-making process in an organization for formulation, implementation and controlling the mission and vision of the organization.

Mangers of the organization become responsible for adapting the organization policy to suit local conditions, their motivation, and accountability to increase efficiency and productivity.

HORIZONTAL DIFFERENTIATION

Horizontal differentiation organization structure as follows:
- Simple structure
- Functional structure
- Divisional structure
- Strategic Business unit
- Matrix structure
- Product team structure
- Geographic structure

SIMPLE STRUCTURE

Simple structure is suitable for small business enterprises. All strategic and operating decisions are centralized in the hands of the owner cum manager. This structure maximizes control by the owner cum manager. Simple structures encourage employee involvement in more than activity.

Merits

It Facilitate to control of all the business activities.

To make rapid decision making and to ability to change with market signals.

It is Simple and informal motivational control systems.

Disadvantages of Simple Structure

It is very demanding on the owner cum manger.

It increasingly inadequate as volume expands.

It does not facilitate the development of future managers.

It tends to focus owner cum manger on day-to-day matters and not on future strategy.

FUNCTIONAL STRUCTURE

Functional structure is the simplest and least expensive in organization design. The Functional structure consists of several functions are as follows:

Finance/accounting

Research and development
Human resource
Marketing
Production
Engineering
Sales and marketing.

Functional structure principally composes of a chief executive officer or a managing director and limited corporate staff with functional line managers in dominant functions like production, accounting, marketing, Research and Development, engineering and human resource. It provides facilities like communication and coordination among the line managers in an organization.

Functional manager's is responsible for formulating and implementing overall corporate strategy and manages divisions via strategic and financial controls.

Advantages
To efficiency through specialization
It is the simplest and less expensive
To improve the development of functional expertise.

To differentiate each division represents a separate business to which the top corporate officer delegates day-to-day operating decisions.

Functional structure promotes specialization of labour, encourages efficiency, minimizes the need for an elaborate control system and allows rapid decision making in an organization.

It is accurately monitoring the performance of individual businesses.

It is simplifying control problems.

It improving the allocation of resource and stimulate mangers of poorly performing divisions to seek ways to improve performance of an organization.

Disadvantages

It promotes narrow specializations and potential functional rivalry or conflict.

It is Difficulty in functional coordination and inters functional decision-making.

It creates staff- line conflict.

It limits internal development of general managers.

Poor delegation of authority

It involves inadequate planning for products and markets

Most of the organizations abandoned the functional structures in favour of decentralization and improved accountability

MULTI-DIVISIONAL STRUCTURE

It is composed of operating divisions where each division represents a separate business in an organization.

Top level officers in an organization delegate's authority to divisional managers to discharge day to day activities.

The Corporate office is responsible for formulating and implementing overall corporate strategy and it manages all divisions via strategic and financial controls.

Multi – division structure was developed in the 1920, the main reasons are listed below:

Functional department difficult to deal with day to day business activities.

Conflict between functional departments to another department.

Costs are not properly allocated individual units.

It is not possible analysis individual product's profit contribution.

Top management becomes over involved in solving short run problems like coordination, communications and conflict management.

New innovative structure issues are outlined:

Creating separate divisions, and each division are representing a distinct process in business.

Each division consists of its functional hierarchy in an organization.

Division managers are responsible persons for day to day business operations in an organization.

Small corporate offices determine the long term strategic direction of the firm and exercise overall control over the multi divisions.

Divisional organizational structure

An organization programme diversifies its product/service line. It covers broad geographic areas and utilized unrelated market channels, or begins to serve distinctly different customer groups and a divisional structure is needed for organization.The divisional structure can be organized in the following manner.

    By geographic area
    By product or service
    By customer
    By process

Divisional Structure by Geographic Area

Divisional structure by geographic area is appropriate for organizations whose strategies are needed to be tailored to fit the particular needs and requirement of customers in different geographic regions in the world.

It is suitable only multinational organization which divisions are dispersed across the world. This type of structure allows local participation in decision making and brings to be improved coordination and cooperation within a region.

Divisional Structure By product or service

This structure most effective for implementing strategies in an organization having specific products and services which are needed special emphasis.

It widely used when an organization offers only a few products and services when its services and products differ substantially.

It allows for strict control over and give attention to product lines for this purpose required skills management force and reduced to top level management control.

Divisional Structure By customer
In this structure, a few customers are vital importance and many different services are provided to these customers, and it is very suitable to implement divisional structure of implementing strategies.

This structure allows an organization to cater effectively to the requirements of clearly defined customer groups. For example, publishing companies often organize their activities around customer's groups like colleges, schools, etc.

Divisional Structure By process

It is similar to a functional structure.

Its activities are organized according to the work, it is actually performed.

Divisional structure by the process is evaluated on the basis of accounting for profit or revenues.

Advantages

It focuses on coordination and necessary authority down to the appropriate level for rapid response.

It should clearly define roles in an each division.

It frees chief executive officer for broader strategic decision-making.

It Places strategy development and implementation in closer proximity to the divisions unique environment.

It sharply focuses accountability for performance.

It retains functional specialization within each division.

It is good training ground for strategic managers.

Division managers are responsible for sales and profit levels in an organization.

It creates career development opportunities for managers and it allows to control of local situations that leads to a competitive climate within the organization and allows new businesses and added to new products easily.

Disadvantages of Divisional Organization Structure

It fosters potentially dysfunctional competition for corporate level resources.

To problem with the extent of authority given to division managers.

To Potential for the policy inconsistencies between divisions.

It problems of arriving at a method to distribute corporate overhead costs that are acceptable to different division managers with profit responsibility.

It is costly due to each division requires functional specialists who must be paid highly salaries because these managers are highly qualified.

Duplication of staff services, facilities and personnel in each division in an organization.

It requires an elaborate, headquarters driven control system.

Divisional structure is not suitable for small firms.

STRATEGIC BUSINESS UNITS

Some organizations encounter difficulty in controlling their divisional operations as the diversity, size, and the number of these units continues to increase. And corporate management may encounter difficulty in evaluating and controlling it's numerous, often multi industry divisions. Under these conditions, it may become necessary to add another layer of management to improve strategy implementation, promotion synergy, and gain greater control over the diverse business interests. It can be achieved by grouping various divisions' in terms of common strategic elements. These groups commonly called strategic business units (SBUs).

It consists of at least three levels, first level is a corporate headquarters at the top, second level is a strategic groups and third level is a divisions grouped by relatedness within each SBU.

It consist of operating units where each unit representing a separate business to which top corporate officer delegates responsibility for day to day operations and business unit strategy to its managers.

It provides for delegation to strategic business unit managers are responsible for the formulation of strategy and implementing appropriate strategies and make proper control for achieving the mission and objectives of an organization.

With in each SBU, divisions are related to each other, and SBU groups are unrelated each other

Advantages of SBUs Organizational Structure

It improves coordination between divisions with similar strategic concerns and product / market environment.

It tightens the strategic management and control of large, diverse business enterprises.

It facilitates distinct and in depth business planning at the corporate and business levels.

It Channels accountability to the distinct business unit.

Strategic business units enable the organization in terms of accurately monitor the performance of individual businesses and simplifying control problems.

It also facilities comparisons between divisions in this way improving the allocation of resource and can be used to stimulate mangers of poorly performing divisions to seek ways to improve performance.

Disadvantages of Strategic Business Unit Organizational Structure

It places another layer of management between the divisions and corporate management.

Its dysfunctional competition for corporate resource may increase.

The role of the group vice president can be difficult to define.

It is the difficulty in defining the degree of autonomy for the group vice presidents and division managers.

MATRIX ORGANIZATIONAL STRUCTURE

The matrix organization provides for dual channels of authority, performance responsibility, evaluation and control. It is essentially; subordinates are assigned to both a basic functional area and a project or product manager. The matrix form is included to combine the advantages of functional specialization and product / project specialization.

In matrix structure, functional and product forms are combined simultaneously at the same level of the organization.

It is the most complex of all designs due to it depends upon both vertical and horizontal flows of authority and communication.

Advantages of Matrix Organizational Structure

It accommodates a wide variety of project oriented business activities.

It provides a good training ground for strategies managers.

It maximizes efficient use of functional managers.

It fosters creativity and multiple sources of diversity.

It is broader middle management exposure to strategic issues for the business.

Its project objectives are very clear in an organization.

It is to be an effective structure for planning, training, clear mutual understanding of roles and responsibilities and mutual trust and confidence.

It is very useful to external environment especially it's technological and market aspects is very complex and changeable.

Disadvantages of Matrix Organizational Structure

It acts as dial accountability can create confusion and contradictory policies.

Necessities tremendous horizontal and vertical coordination.

It produces conflicts revolving around duties, authority and resource allocation.

Its goals are vague and technology used in a project that is poorly understood.

Old Organization Design

It is one and large corporation

It requires vertical communication

It is needed centralized top down decision making

It involves quality teams

It as a functional work teams

It requires minimal training

It specialized job design focused on individual

It is vertical integration

New Organizational Design

It requires horizontal communication

It is decentralized

It involves autonomous work teams

It as cross functional work teams

It needs extensive training

It is a value chain team focused job redesign

It is outsourcing and virtual organizations

DEVELOPMENT OF MATRIX STRUCTURE

Davis and Lawrence have proposed three distinct phases for development of matrix structure.

Cross – Functional task forces
Product / Brand management
Mature Matrix

Cross Functional Task Force

It is temporary cross functional forces which are initially used when a new product line is being introduced in an organization.

In this task force, the project manager is in charge as the key horizontal link.

Product / Brand Management

In the cross functional task forces become more permanent, the project manager becomes a product or brand manager and a second phase begins.

In this arrangement, it is primary organizational structure, but in this case, product brand or brand mangers act as the integrators of semi permanent products or brands in an organization.

Mature Matrix

It is the third and final phase of matrix development involves a true deal authority structure in an organization.

In this case, both the functional and product structures are permanent.

All employees in organization connect to both a vertical functional superior and horizontal product manager.

In this mature structure, functional and product managers have equal authority and must work well together to resolve disagreements over resources and priorities.

Product Team Structure

Product team structure is a major structural innovation in recent years. It has similar advantages to a matrix structure but is much easier and for less costly to operate because of the way people are organized into permanent cross-functional teams.

GEOGRAPHIC STRUCTURE

The Company operates as a geographic structure, geographic regions become the basis for the grouping of organizational activities. For instance, a company may divide its manufacturing operations and establish manufacturing plants in different regions of the country. Service organizations like store chains or banks may organize their sales marketing activities on a regional, rather than national level to get closer to their customer.

The Geographic structure provides more control than a functional structure because there are several regional hierarchies carrying out the work previously performed by a single centralized hierarchy.

CHAPTER 6
INTEGRATION AND INTEGRATING MECHANISMS

The level of integration and integrating mechanisms are necessary for organizational structure to work effectively and efficiently. Integration refers to the extent to which an organization seeks to coordinate its value creation activities and make them independent. The design issues can be summed up simply the higher a company's level of differentiation, the higher level integration is needed to make organizational structure work efficiently. Therefore, the company only integrates its task activities to the extent necessary to implement its strategy effectively and efficiently.

TYPES / FORMS OF INTEGRATING MECHANISMS

Forms / types of integrating mechanisms of the company can be used to increase its level of integration. Types / forms of integrating mechanisms are listed below:

Direct contact
Liaison roles
Task forces
Teams
Integrating roles
Integrating departments
Matrix

Direct Contact

Chief executive officer has directly contacted among managers from different divisions or functional department can work together to solve mutual problems. Different functions managers have tended to equal authority for the accomplishment of goals and objectives of the organization with cooperation and motivation.

Interdepartmental Liaison Roles

A company has improved its efficiency by through of interdepartmental liaison roles of among managers in the organization. When the volume of contact is increased two or more departments, its result is improved the cooperation and coordination. Therefore, functional managers are contacting among managers of organization, weekly, monthly. It builds up healthy relationships among employees of the company.

Temporary Task Forces

Task force involves the planning and solutions of the difficult and complex problems. It arises from different functional departments of the company. The Task force is a just like committee. It is committed to the solution of the problems of the organization. The Task force is temporary, therefore, once the problem is solved, members of the task force should return to their normal roles in their departments or are assigned to other task forces. Task force members also perform many of their normal duties while serving on the task force.

Permanent teams

Task force solves the problems effectively and efficiently an organization must establish permanent integrating mechanisms like as a permanent team. Example – product development committee.

Integrating Roles

Integrating roles means, a functional /divisions mangers job is a full time. Who is normally a senior manager with a great deal of experience in the joint needs of the two departments? The job is to coordinate the decision process among departments/ divisions so that the synergetic gains from cooperation can be obtained.

Integrating Department

The permanent integrating department is established at corporate head quarters. This department consists of mainly of strategic planners and may indeed be called the strategic planning department. Corporate head quarter's staffs in a divisional structure can also be viewed as an integrating department from the divisional perspective.

Matrix Structure

Lastly, differentiation is high and the company must be able to respond quickly to the environment, a matrix structure becomes the appropriate integrating device.

Institutionalizing the strategy

Three organizational elements provide the fundamental and long term for institutionalizing the company' strategy are as follows:

Structure
Leadership
Culture

MATCHING STRUCTURE AND CONTROL ANALYSIS AT THE FUNCTIONAL LEVEL

Matching structure and control analysis strategy at the functional level are as below:

Manufacturing functions/divisions
Research and development functions/divisions
Marketing division/functions
Human resource division
Accounting and finance division
Customer welfare division
Production departments

These are the matching structure of the functional level.

MATCHING STRUCTURE AND CONTROL AT THE BUSINESS LEVEL

Matching structure and control at the business level are as below:

Generic business level strategies

Cost leadership strategy and structure

Differentiation strategy and structure

Implementing a combined differentiation and cost leadership strategy

Focus strategy and structure

These are the matching structure of the business level.

DESIGNING A GLOBAL STRUCTURE

Global structure is consisting of the following areas:

Multi domestic strategy and structure

International strategy and structure

Global strategy and structure

Transnational strategy and structure

MULTIDOMESTIC STRATEGY AND STRUCTURE

A company pursues a multi domestic strategy; it generally operates business with a global area structure.

Global Area Structure

A company duplicates all values like value creation activities and establishes a foreign decision in every country or world in which it operates. Authority can be decentralized to mangers in each foreign division and they devise the appropriate strategy for responding to the needs of the local environment. Corporate head quarter is much farther away from the scene of operations. It makes sense to decentralize, control and grant decision authority to managers in foreign operations. Mangers at global headquarters use market and output controls as listed:

Rate of return

Growth in market share

Operation costs evaluate the **performance of foreign divisions.**

On the basis of these comparisons in global level and they can make global capital allocation decisions and global transfer of new technical knowledge.

INTERNATIONAL STRATEGY AND STRUCTURE

A company has adopted an international strategy to enter into international market for global expansion. Normally, the company shifts to this strategy when it begins selling its domestically made products in foreign markets.

As a separate divisional business with International operations. International company has provided the authority and responsibility to managers in coordinating domestic product divisions and foreign market. The international division also controls the foreign subordinate, market the products and decides how much authority to delegate to foreign management.

GLOBAL ORGANISATIONAL STRUCTUE

Growing of international business operations and increasing of business competitive environment. Its result is a global organizational structure. It further classified into five categories. They are as follows:

Global products structure
Global area structure
Global functional structure
Global customer structure
Hybrid / mixed structure
Global Product Structure

The worldwide product structure is based upon major product groups.

Global product structure responsibilities are involved in all functions for marketing a specific product group or class throughout the world. It can be delegated to a group within each product division. Therefore, there is a corporate staff at the headquarters to provide wide expertise and provide some degree of assistance to each product division; the product divisions have a good deal of autonomy with their own functional staff.

Company's international activities like product-oriented structure are allocated among the various product divisions. Therefore, the significance of the overseas operations varies substantially. Some of the firm's products maybe more amenable to export or import markets than others or the management of some division may simply have more international experience than does managers in other divisions.

The global product structure has the advantage of focusing upon and optimizing the firm's production strengths. The managers of different product divisions have developed a

great deal of knowledge that relates to the following:
- Products
- Competitors
- Production facilities
- Market
- Customer characteristics

They develop familiarity with the environmental constraints of products and how best to position these products in various markets for a variety of users. The product managers can also develop a worldwide perspective regarding sales and marketing for their groups.

Advantages of Global Product Structure

This structure suitable for firms with very diverse product lines catering to very different end users in different distributional channels.

The great diversity of the firm's products, end users and distribution channels are the most attractive.

Disadvantages of Global Product Structure

Global structure suffers from manifold weakness.

Its absence of central international focus there maybe lack of communication and coordination among different the product division.

Duplication of operational efficiency and often creating confusion among customers.

Corporate management actively encourages international development, not all product divisional mangers may be interested in developing their overseas potential.

THE GLOBAL AREA STRUCTURE

This form of global organization is based on upon a geographical orientation, either the geographical location of customers or of the company's productive facility. It indicates the global area structure. The firm is organized on the basis of geographical areas of its international markets. The configuration of the geographical structure depends on the markets in which a multinational corporation operates but typical divisions occur according to major market areas like India, North America, Europe, Middle East, and South America. Under the global area structure, all of the firm's activities relating to any products or service that is bought, sold or produced within a region, are under the control of the regional group head who reports directly to the president of the firm.

Advantages of the Global Area Structure

This form of organization follows the marketing concept in as much as individual areas and markets are given concentrated attention.

Geographical -oriented corporate structure, a multinational firm can place greater emphasis on the specific needs, market characteristics and market requirements of the individual market areas. The firm can pay concentrated attention to satisfy local demands and there by improve its market share

The Global Area Structure
Disadvantages of the Global Area Structure

The major weakness of this form of global organization is that by emphasizing regional operations, it fails to facilitate the development of the coordination of functional or product line activity worldwide.

The firm misses the opportunity of economies of scale introduction or in raw materials sourcing.

Its failure to learn the regional operation of the organization factors like as production, development, and marketing on a global basis.

Another drawback to this type of structure is that it requires the allocation of considerable resources to establish regional headquarter headed by area managers

There are certain problems involved in this form of structure. It involves duplication of specialists in the different divisions, since such services are not centralized in the geographically structured company.

The geographical orientation tends to give the mangers in such group a geographical rather than a companywide perspective.

The Global Functional Structures

Under this structure, global operations of the firm are organized primarily on a functional basis. This figure indicates the global functional structure.

Advantages of Global functional structures

This structure has the economies of scale gained within each functional area.

Duplication of expert service is kept to a minimum with consequent savings in manpower.

Functional form of organizational structure finds favor with multinational firms having a narrow range of products and homogenous markets around the world.

Disadvantages of Global functional structures

Problem of coordination between functions or divisions of the company.

Lack of flexibility for a firm attempting to market a number of products in a number of markets

Mangers in this form organization develop too narrow a perspective in emphasizing their own functions rather than the overall welfare of the company.

The Global Customer Structures

Sometimes firms may organize its global operations according to the customer goods. The global customer structures as listed below:

Individuals
Business
Governments

Corporate staff provided the most specialized and personalized service. Therefore, however, it also tends to require duplication of skills in each group and a separation between such specialists in each group. However, corporate staff can reduce some of these disadvantages but can never totally overcome them.

Global Matrix Structure

This structure makes it very difficult for the different product groups to trade information and knowledge and obtain the benefits of corporation. Sometimes the potential gains from sharing product, marketing and research development knowledge between product groups are very high.

Global Matrix Structure

Matrix structures work help to companies to develop a strong international organizational culture to facilitate communication and coordination among managers.

Network Structures

It newer and radical organization design.

Network structures involve many activities are outsourced to partners.

It is consisting of a series of project groups or collaborations lined by constantly changing non hierarchical and cobweb like networks.

When a firm environment is unstable that time this network is useful to an organization.

Network organization structures consist of a series of independent firms or business linked together by computers in an information an information system that designs, produces and markets a product or services.

Advantages

It provides an organization with increased flexibility and adaptability to cope with rapid technological change and shifting patterns of international trade a competition thereby enhances their strengths.

It allows to company to concentrate on its distinctive competencies to provide services to their client.

Net working firms are supplying the skill and trained employees to their clients and achieve client's mission and vision.

Networking companies have provided services through contract with the client.

It arrangement of newly evolving that typically are in response to social and technological advances.

Disadvantages

The availability of numerous potential partners can be a source of trouble to networking companies.

Some time agreement is failure due to unable provide services and want to separate suppliers or distributors may keep the firm from discovering any synergies by combining activities.

Few networking companies are offering highly specialize few functions only, so that it is also disadvantages of network companies.

This type of companies runs the risk of choosing the wrong functions and thus it become noncompetitive.

STRATEGIC BUSINESS UNITS AND CORE COMPETENCE

Strategic business units and core competence are outlined as:

Strategic business units are playing significant role in multinational organization.

Most of the modern organizations are organized their business into appropriate strategic business units in world.

It is the relevant, suitable to multiproduct and multibusiness enterprise.

It provides separate strategic planning treatment for each one of its products and businesses.

It is a grouping of related business activities in an enterprise that is amenable to composite planning treatment to all business activities in an organization.

In scientific sense, it is a multibuisness enterprise group its multitude of businesses into a few distinct business units.

It is to provide effective strategic planning treatment to each one of its products or business offered by an enterprise.

Strategic business unit's firms are handling business planning on a territorial basis since their structure was territorial; this structure is the outcome of a manufacturing or distribution logistics.

Characteristics of Strategic Business Units

There are three most important characteristics of strategic business units are outlined:

It is a single business or collection of related businesses which offer scope for independent planning and that feasibly stand alone from the rest of the organization.

It has own set of competitors in the market.

Strategic mangers in SBUs who has responsibility for strategic planning and profit performance and control of unnecessary activities which are harmful to strategic business units.

Strategic Business Units Planning Difficulties

Strategic business units in territory planning rise to two kinds of difficulties are listed below:

A number of territorial units handled the same products; the same product was getting varied strategic planning treatments in an enterprise.

A given territorial planning unit carried different and unrelated products, products and dissimilar characteristics are getting identical strategic planning treatment in the organization

Concepts of Strategic Business Units

It is underlying the grouping principle that relates all products and services falling under one strategic business units.

It helps to a multibusinesss corporation in scientifically grouping its businesses into a few distinct business process units.

It provides the right direction to strategic planning by removing the vague and confusion often experienced in multibusiness grouping enterprise.

Strategic Business Units and Its Benefits

Strategic business units help to with organization for strategic planning that is based on the scientific method of grouping the business activities.

It brings improvement in territorial grouping of business and these units based on strategic planning.

It is the grouping of related businesses which can be taken into for strategic planning that distinct from the rest of the business. Each unit in strategic groups will be getting equal priority among the products and services in an organization.

It task is relating to anglicizing and segregating the assortment of business or portfolios and regrouping them into few, well defined, distinct and scientifically demarcated business unit. If product or businesses are related from the standpoint of 'function' are assembled together as consider as distinct SBUs.

In the case, unrelated products, businesses is any group are separated from the main business, if they assigned to any other SBU that applying the criterion of functional relation, these are assigned accordingly. Otherwise, these are made into separate SBUs.

It is removing the vagueness and confusion from the strategic business units and its products and services in an enterprise.

It also provides the right facilities to set correct strategic planning to each unit in strategic business units.

SBU is separate businesses from the strategic planning point of view. It means each strategic business units mission, objectives, competition, and strategy will be distinct from one to another.

Each strategic units will have own set of competitors and its own distinct strategy in an enterprise.

Each SBU CEO is responsible for strategic planning for their Strategic business unit and its performance in terms of profitability, growth, development and also considers controlling factors in an organization.

Strategic Issues in Strategic Business Units

Strategic issues in strategic business units at corporate levels are first whether the corporate body wishes to have a related set of SBUs or not and if so, on what basis. Strategic issues are relatedness in turn has direct implications on decisions about diversification relatedness may exist in different ways as listed way:

Strategic business units may build on similar technologies or all provide similar sorts of products and services offered to customers.

It can be served with a similar or different market even if different technologies or products and different customer.
Competences and competitive advantages in SBUs are different and similar to strategic business units.

CHAPTER 7
THE VALUE CHAIN

INTRODUCTION

The primary analytical tool of value chain is identifying the separate activities, functions and business process of the organization that are performed in designing, producing, marketing, delivering and supporting a product and service. The chain of value is creating activities like, it takes to provide a product or service activities that starts with raw materials supply and continues on through conversion of the raw material into finished product or service, after the distribution of goods and service to ultimate user of the product or service.

BASIC CONCEPT OF VALUE CHAIN

A company's or organization value chain identifies the primary activities and supporting activities create the value for end user of the product and service.

The value chain of the organization creates the value for the product and service. It is measured by the amount that buyers are willing to pay for a product or service. Organization is profitable, it creates exceeds the value for the product or service. The value creation functions are as listed below:

General administration
Operations,
Material management
Research and Development
Human resource
Infrastructures
Procurement
Marketing

These functions gain to competitive advantage of an organization. Company or organization must perform value creation functions at a lower cost.

THE VALUE CREATION PROCESS

The value creation process chain concept popularized by Michael Porter.

Value creation process is classified into two types. They are as follows:

Primary Activities
Supporting Activities

It is also knowing that company value chain. The company value chain consists of the primary activities and the supporting activities of the company. Company value chain activities are as listed below:

PRIMARY ACTIVITIES
Primary activities are as outlined:
Purchased supplies and inbound logistics
Operations
Distribution and outbound logistics
Sales and marketing
Services

Purchased Supplies and Inbound Logistics
Purchased supplies and inbound logistics activities are as outlined:
Activities
Costs
Assets associated with purchasing fuel
Raw materials
Past components
Merchandise and consumable items from vendors

Receiving, storing and disseminating inputs from suppliers, inspection

Inventory management

Operations

Operations activities are as below:
Activities

Costs and assets associated with converting inputs into final product form (production, assembly, packing, equipment, maintenance, facilities, operations, quality assurance, and environmental protection.)

The operation management functions can controls the transmission of physical materials through the value chain from procurement through operations and into distribution. The efficiency is carried out can lower the cost of value creation. Further, an effective operation management function can monitor the quality of inputs into the manufacturing process.

Distribution and outbound Logistics

Distribution and outbound logistics are as listed below:
Activities
Costs

Assets dealing with physically distributing the product to buyers (finished goods warehousing, order processing, order picking and packing, shipping, delivery vehicle operations, establishing and maintaining a network of dealers and distributors).

Sales and Marketing
Sales and marketing activities are as listed below:
Activities
Costs
Assets related to sales force efforts
Advertising and promotion market research and planning
Dealer/distribution support

Service
Service activities are as outlined:
Activities
Costs
Assets associated with providing assistance to buyers such as installation, spare parts delivery, maintenance and repair, technical assistance, buyers inquire and complaints.

SUPPORTING ACTIVITIES
supporting activities of the company

or organization also known as cross functional goals and value chain. Supporting activities are known as functional activities of the organization. Supporting activities are as listed below:

Research, Technology and Systems Development
Human resource management
General administration
Efficiency
Quality
Innovation
Customer responsiveness

Support Activities

Support activities are listed below:
Research, technology and systems delivered
Human resource management
General administration

Research, Technology and Systems Delivered

Research, technology and systems delivered are essential requirement of the company. Research, technology and systems delivered are as outlined.
Activities
Costs and assets relating to product R&D,

Process R&D
Process design improvements
Equipment design
Computer software development
Telecommunications system
Computer assisted designs and engineering
New data base capabilities
Development of computerized support systems.

The R&D function develops new product and its process technologies. Technological innovation result is lower manufacturing costs and result in the creation of more attractive products that demand a premium price. It can affect primary manufacturing and marketing activities, and through them value creation.

Human Resources Management

Human resources management refers to recruitment, hiring, training, development and compensation of the employees of the organization. Human resource management activities are as follows:

Activities
Costs
Assets associated with the recruitment, hiring training,

development, and compensation of all types of personnel.

Labor relations activities

Developed of knowledge based skills and core competencies.

The human resource function ensures that the company or organization has the right mix of skill people to perform its value creation activities effectively.

General Administration

General administration refers to administration of the organization. The general administration activities are as listed below:

Activities

Costs

Assets relating to general management

Accounting and finance

Legal and regulatory affairs

Safety and security

Management information systems

Forming strategic alliances and collaborating with strategic partners and other overhead d functions.

Infrastructure is the final supporting activities of the company or organization value chain.It has a somewhat different character from the other support activities. Infrastructure is the company's or organization wide context within which all the other value creation activities take place. It includes the company's or organizational structure, control systems, and culture.

Value creation activities are as Superior efficiency, quality; innovation and customer responsiveness are achieving goals of the company or organization. These activities are requires strategies for formulation, implementation and monitor, guide and controlling of value chain activities of the organization or company.

Steps in Value Chain Analysis
Value chain analysis can be broken down into a three sequential steps are as follows:

Break down a market/organization into its key activities under each of the major headings in the model.

Assess the potential for adding value via cost advantage or differentiation, or identify current activities where a business appears to be at a competitive disadvantage.

Determine strategies built around focusing on activities where competitive advantage can be sustained.

CHAPTER 8
CONCEPT OF CORPORATE CULTURE

INTRODUCTION

A concept of corporate culture refers to the following factors:
- A company's values
- Beliefs
- Business principles
- Traditions
- Ways of operating
- Internal environment of the company
- Assumptions
- Norms
- Rules and regulations
- Policies and procedure of the corporate

CORPORATE CULTURE

Corporate culture is the set of important assumptions. Every company has its own culture it's followed by all the members of the company. Corporate culture is similar to an individual's personality, principles, concept and trade practice ethical opinion actions within the company or organization.

BASIC ELEMENTS OF CORPORATE CULTURE

Organization culture is the set of important assumptions are sufficiently central to the life of the organization or company. Basic elements of corporate culture are as listed below:

Basic Assumptions and Beliefs
Cultural artifacts
Values
Norms

BASIC ASSUMPTIONS AND BELIEFS

Basic assumptions and beliefs are important to the corporate world. In addition to know, how it actually works, basic assumptions and beliefs derive from personal experience and are reinforced by it in the company. Corporate staff is relying to some degree on the judgment and expertise of others this based on the basic assumptions and beliefs. They trust or can identify with to help them and to decide what to believe or not believe. It underpins the various aspects of organizational activity and represents the core ideology of the business. Some examples of the basic assumptions and beliefs underlying organizational culture:

Market oriented communication system

Customer orientation

Employee participation, open communication and security

Entrepreneurism, self discipline and control

Cultural Artifacts

Cultural artifacts are the visible manifestation of culture. It reflects in the physical and social environment of the organization like its structure systems, subsystems, symbol and plaques etc., an important cultural artifacts are public documents, media reports and stories about the organization, its rituals, ceremonies, rules, procedures and observable behavior of its members. Therefore, these cultural artifacts form a system of support and maintenance of the set of prevailing beliefs.

Values

Values refer to the conception of what members of an organization regard as desirable. They are the deep-rooted feelings about ideas and physiology, desires and preferences, emotions and beliefs that influence the members' reaction and responses to any situation. Corporate culture involves shared values, social ideals, or normative beliefs about proper behavior in various situations. Organizational values are reflected in terms of beliefs, emotions, desires, preferences and behaviors of the members of the organization. It stated reasons therefore, in neutral value, orientation emotions are not expressed freely. However, organizations are having affective value generation and encourage free expressions among the people and the groups. In specific value orientation interactions between people, are direct, purposeful, precise, and transparent and authority relationship are confined to work situation. Organizations are espousing the diffuse value that encourages maintaining relationships among the organizational people outside the organization also.

Norms

Norms are the paradigms, the informal rules of the game telling employees what they are supposed to be saying, believing, and doing and what is right and what is wrong. For example, as per the IBM norms employees should attentively listen to their demands. Norms are generally passed on to new employees by word of mouth and enforced by the social approval or disapproval of one's behavior in terms of its congruence or in congruence with prevalent norms.

CONTENTS OF CORPORATE CULTURE

Corporate culture contents that ultimately derive from three major sources are as follows:

It influences the business environment in general and the industry in specifically.

Founders, leaders, directors and corporate employees bring a systematic pattern of assumptions with them when they join the corporate world. These assumptions are dynamic in terms of personal experience, regional, ethnic, religious, occupational and professional communities from which they came.

Realty and experience of human resource of the corporate world to make and use the solution and coping with the basic problems of the corporate culture world.

STRENGTHS OF CORPORATE CULTURE

The strength of a culture has influenced the intensity by which organization members comply with it as they go about their day-to-day activities. The specific feature of culture that determine the basic strengths of corporate culture are as follows:

- Strong culture companies
- Weak culture companies
- Unhealthy culture
- Adaptive culture
- Thickness culture
- Extent of sharing culture
- Clarity of ordering culture

Strong Culture Companies

A strong culture is a valuable asset when it matches strategy and dreaded liability when it does not. Strong culture companies refer to company conduct its business according to clear and explicit set of principles and values. Strong culture is the strength and one of the features of the culture. Therefore, strong culture companies typically have creeds or values statements and executives regularly stress the importance of using these values and principles as the basis for decisions and actions taken throughout the organization. There are three important factors contribute to the development of strong culture factors. They are as listed below:

A founder or strong leader who establishes values, principles and practice that are consistent and sensible insight of customer needs, competitive conditions and strategic requirements of the business.

A sincere, long standing company commitment to operating the business according to these established traditions, thereby creating an internal environment that supports decision-making and strategies based on the cultural norms.

A generic concern for the well-being of the organization's three biggest constituencies like customers, employees and shareholders. Continuity of leadership, small group rise, stable group membership, geographic concentration and considerable organizational success all contribute to the emergence and sustainability of a strong culture.

Weak Culture Companies

Weak culture companies refers to company culture, there is little cohesion and glue across organization units – top executives don't repeatedly expose any business philosophy or exhibit commitment to particular values or extoll uses of particular operating practices. Because of a dearth of common values and ingrained business approaches. Organization members typically have no deeply felt senses of corporate identity. In weak culture there are no traditions, beliefs, values, common bonds or behavioral norms. It provides little or no strategy implementation assistance that the management can use as levers to mobilize commitment to executing the chooses strategy.

Unhealthy Cultures

Unhealthy culture refers to companies they are adopted number of unhealthy cultural characteristics which can undermine a company's business performance. Unhealthy culture characteristics are as follows:

A political internal environment allows and influencing mangers to operate autonomous 'fiefdoms' and resist needed change.

The second unhealthy cultural trait, one that can plague companies suddenly confronted with fast changing business conditions, is hostility to change and to people who champion new ways of doing things.

Unhealthy characteristic is promoting mangers who are good at staying within their budgets, exerting close supervisory control over their units can handling administrative detail as opposed to mangers who understand vision, strategies and culture building and who are good leaders, motivators and decision makers.

The last trait of unhealthy culture is a version to looking outside the company for superior practices and approaches.

Adaptive Culture

Adaptive culture is a valuable competitive asset. Sometimes is a necessity for organization; in fast changing environments for instance, today's dot com companies are classic example of adaptive culture.

In adaptive cultures, members share of confidence that the organization can deal with whatever threats and opportunities come down the pike:they are receptive to risk taking, experimentation, innovation, and changing strategies and proactive whenever necessary to satisfy the legitimate interests of stakeholders, customers employees, shareowners, suppliers and the communities where the company operates.

Thickness culture

Thick cultures have many, thin culture has few cultures with many layers of implement shared beliefs and values generally have a stronger influence behavior.

Extent of Sharing culture

Some of important assumptions are more widely shared than others. Few are completely shared in the sense that every members of the organization has internalized them. Culture with more widely shared beliefs and value has a more pervasive impact because they guide more people.

Clearly or Ordering culture

Some organizational cultures the shared beliefs and values are clearly ordered. Cultures whose shared assumptions are clearly ordered have a more pronounced effect on behavior because members of the organization are sure of which values should prevail incases of conflicting interests.

Deciphering a Culture

Reading a culture is an interpretive subjective activity. One cannot decipher a culture simply by relying on what people say about it other evidence, both historical and current, must be taken into account to infer the culture.

The frame work for deciphering culture is presented systematic method to help decipher or infer an organization culture. Each important shared assumption creating an organizations culture may be inferred from one or more shared things, shared sayings and feelings, the important point is to distill from these various cultural manifestations a much more concise set of important shared beliefs and values.

HOW CULTURE INFLUENCES ORGANISATIONAL

We need to examine five basic processes that lie at the heart of any

organization - they are as outlined below:
- Cooperation
- Decision making
- Control
- Communication
- Commitment

Cooperation

Cooperation is the important tool for mangers to cope with solutions of the problems in the internal environment. Management to take carefully contracted with the external world in terms of maintaining very good relationship to improvement of the efficiency and increased productivity of the corporate culture.

Decision Making

Organizational culture affects the decision making process because shared beliefs and values give organizational members a consistent set of basic assumptions and preferences. It leads to a more efficient decision making process.

Control

The essence of control is the ability to take action to achieve planned results. The basic for action is provided by two different control mechanisms are as follows:

Formal procedure

Clans

Formal Procedures

Formal procedures rely on adjusting rules, procedures, guidelines, budgets, and directives.

Clans

The clan's mechanism relies on shared beliefs and values. In effect, shared beliefs and values constitutes on organizational 'compass' that members rely on to choose appropriate course of action clan control derives from culture.

A strong culture facilitates the control process by enhancing clan control. Clan control is highly efficient, but again, efficiency and effectiveness should not be confused.

Communication

Communication should be clear and clarity to understand by one person to another i.e. communication. Corporate culture reduces these dangers of miscommunication into ways are as follows:

There is no need to communicate in matters for which shared assumptions already exist.

Shared assumptions provide guidelines and cues to help interpret messages that are received.

Therefore, a strong culture encourages efficient and effective communication. Communication is the lifeblood of organizations.

Commitment

A person feels committed to an organization when he or she identifies with it and experiences some emotional attachment to it. A variety of incentives like as salary, prestige, and personal sense of worth. Strong culture encourages efficient and effective commitments.

Building Ethics into culture

An ethical corporate culture has a positive impact on a company's long-term strategic success; an unethical culture can undermine it. Values and ethical standards must not only be explicitly stated but must also be ingrained into the corporate culture.

Implementing the values and code of ethics entails the following actions:

To incorporation of the statement of values and the code of ethics in employee training and educational programmes.

To explicitly attention to values and ethics in recruiting and hiring to screen out applicants who don't exhibit compatible character traits.

To communication of the values and ethics code to all employees and explaining compliance procedures.

To management involvement and oversight from CEO down to first line supervisors.

To word of mouth indoctrination

To strong endorsements by the CEO.

CHAPTER 9

STRATEGIC LEADERSHIP

INTRODUCTION

Strategic manager has to play significant different leadership role as listed below:

Visionary
Chief entrepreneurial and strategist
Chief administrator and strategy implementer
Culture builder
Resource acquirer and allocator
Capabilities builder
Process integrator
Coach crisis solver
Task master
Spokesperson
Negotiator
Motivator
Arbitrator
Consensus builder
Policy maker
Policy enforcer
Mentor
And head cheer leader

Some times, it is useful to be authoritarian and hardnosed;

sometimes it is best to be a perceptive listener and a compromising decision maker, sometimes strong participative, collegial approach works best; and sometimes being a coach and adviser is the proper role.

Strategic leader act as many occasions call for a highly visible role and extensive time commitments. While others entailed a brief ceremonial performance with the details delegated to subordinates.

Strategic Mangers have five leadership roles to play in pushing for good strategy execution is as follows:

He has closely monitoring progress of the top management and studies the overall changes in organization for this purpose he is learning what obstacles lies in the path of good execution.

To promote a culture and esprit de corps that mobilizes and energizes organizational members to execute strategy in a competent fashion and perform at high level.

To keep the organization respond to changing conditions alert for new opportunities, bubbling with innovative ideas, and ahead of rivals in developing competitively valuable competencies and capabilities.

To exercise ethics leadership and insisting that the company conduct its affair like a model corporate citizen.

To push corrective actions to improve strategy execution and overall strategic performance.

LEADERSHIP ROLE IN IMPLEMENTATION

The Leadership role is vital for the formulation, implementation and control of strategy in an organization. Leadership roles are provided new opportunities, challenges, development of existing and new strategies in an organization. Strategic leaders are effective and able to use the strategic management process to design the strategic programme for the formulation of strategy and implementation of strategy in an organization.

It highlights the strategy design and implementation with the interrelationship of elements like organization, information system, management control, reward system, management development, and environment at scanning, strategic planning, policy formulation and get feedback.

Strategic leadership focus on the ability to anticipate, envision, maintain flexibility and manpower to be used for design strategic programme.

Strategic leader should exhibit skills like ability to guide an organization, analysis of competitive scenario in the market, how to buildup effective team and strategic groups for accomplishment mission and vision.

To know how to tackle changes in the different environment scenario.

To cooperate and cooperation among the human resource in an organization.

To take feedback and forecast to future and its result.

To posses modern skills like technical , human , conceptual skills and to know when to use these skills for proper control in an organization issues like expansion of business, mergers, acquisition and strategic alliance and diversification of business activities.

Strategic manager's ability to manage human skills and critical task in an organization.

EFFECTIVE STRATEGIC LEADERSHIP

Strategic leaders are those who refers to top management in an organization, it consists of a board of directors and chief executive officer in company and also consist of strategic business units division managers in an organization.

Strategic leaders are defining mission and vision, frame the strategy and its choice, and take initiative to implement the appropriate strategy and achieve action oriented results.

Strategic Leaders Responsibilities

Strategic leader's responsibilities are listed below:

Effectively managing the human resource and effectively and efficiently managed firm's business operations.

To sustain high level achievement in terms of profit, growth and expansion of business activities in firms.

To make bold and planned, organized decisions for accomplishment major tasks in enterprise.

To make effective feedback via face to face communications in enterprise.

Decision making responsibilities which cannot be delegated.

Two leadership issues in an organization

The role of the chief executive officers (CEO)

The assignment of key managers

STRATEGIC LEADERS

Role of Strategic CEO

The chief executive officer is the catalyst in strategic management. CEO is most closely identified with and ultimately accountable for a strategy's success. In most corporate world, particularly larger ones, CEOs spend into 80 percent of their time developing and guiding strategy.

The nature of the CEO role is both a symbolic and substantive in strategy implementation as follows:

The CEO is a symbol of the new strategy. CEO actions and the perceived seriousness of his other commitment to a choosen strategy, particularly if the strategy represents a major change, except a significant influence on the intensity of subordinate mangers commitment to implementation.

The organization mission, strategy and key long term objectives are strongly influenced by the personal goals and values of its CEO. To the extent that the CEO invests time and personal values in the chosen strategy. He or she represents an important source for clarification, guidance and adjustment during implementation.

Major changes in strategy are often quality followed by a change in CEO. Successful strategy implementations directly linked to the unique characteristics, orientations and actions of the CEO

Key consideration in managerial assignments to implement strategy

A new strategy Subject Issue Using the Existing executives to to implement

Advantages

Already know key people, Practice and conditions.

Personal qualities better known and understand by associates.

Have established relationships with peers, subordinates, suppliers, etc

Symbolizes organizational commitment to individual Careers.

Disadvantages

Less adaptable to Major strategic Changes because of knowledge, attitudes and values.

Past commitments May hamper hard decisions required in executing a new strategy

Less ability to Become inspired and credibly conveys the need for change.

Bringing Outsiders to Implement a new strategy

Advantages

Outsiders may already
Believe Inland have "lived"
The new Strategy
Outsider is unencumbered
By internal commitments to people
Outsiders come to the
New assignment with
Heightened commitment and enthusiasm.

Bringing is an outsider can send powerful signals throughout the organization that change is expected.

Disadvantages
Often costly, both
In terms of compensation and
Learning to work together
Time.

Candidates suitable in all respects (Exact experience) may not Be available leading to compromise choices.

Uncertainty in Selecting the right person.

The "morale" costs When an outsider takes a job Several insiders wanted.

"What to do with poorly Free problems"

FOUR MANAGERIAL ASSIGNMENT SITUATIONS

Four managerial assessment situations are
Selective blend
Turnover
Stability
Reorientations

Selective blend

Current executives via promotion and transfer where skills match
New roles; otherwise seek skills and experience via outsiders.

Turnover
Outsiders should be a high priority to provide new Skills motivational, and enthusiasm.

Stability
Current executives and Internal promotions should be Major emphasis in order to Reward, retain, and develop

Turnover
Outsiders should be A high priority to provide new Skills motivational, and enthusiasm. Managerial talent

Reorientations
Outsiders are important To replace weaknesses and Communication seriousness "Current executive should be a Priority where possible via Promotion transfer or role clarification

CHAPTER 10

STRATEGIC CONTROL SYSTEMS

INTRODUCTION

We shall examine the main operational control system; monitoring performance and evaluating deviations, strategic control systems allow top managers to monitor and evaluate the performance of divisions, functions, and employees and to take corrective action to improve their performance. Strategic control is the process of establishing the appropriate types of control system at the corporate, business and functional levels in a company which allow the strategic mangers for guiding and evaluating the strategy in the organization.

Control strategy can be characterized as a form of 'steering control' ordinarily, a significant time span occurs between the initial implementation of a strategy and achievement of its intended results. During that time, numerous projects are undertaken, investments are made, and actions are undertaken to implement the new strategy. In addition, during that time, both the environmental situation and firm's internal situation are developing and evolving. Strategic control is necessary to steer the firm through these events. They must provide the basis for correcting the actions and directions of the firm in implementing its strategy to development and changes in its environment and internal situation take place.

STRATEGIC CONTROL SYSTEM

Strategic control systems are vital aspects of implementing the strategy of an organization. The primary function of strategic control systems is to provide information for management. Information needs to control its strategy and structure. Strategic control systems are the formal target setting, monitoring, and evaluation and feedback systems. It provides information to management about the organization's strategy and structure. Both are meeting strategic performance and mission and vision of an organization.

CHARACTERISTICS OF STRATEGIC CONTROL SYSTEMS

It should be providing accurate information and is giving a true picture of organizational performance.

It should be flexible enough to allow managers to respond as necessary to un expected events in organization.

It should supply information to managers in a timely sense.

Process / Steps in Designing an Effective Control System in organisation

There are four stages involved in designing an effective control system of an organization. They are as follows:

Establish standards and targets

Create measuring and monitoring system

Compare actual performance against the established targets

Evaluate results and take action if necessary

Establish Standards and Targets

Establish standard and targets is the first stage in design an effective control system. Company managers select standard targets to evaluate its performance. Standard targets are major objectives and goals of the company. It is accomplished and monitoring by managers of company or organization.

Create Measuring and Monitoring Systems

This is the second stage of establishing strategic control systems. Company has established procedures for assessing work goals at all levels in the organization. Either work goal achieved or not achieved. Organization task is the difficult task to measure and monitoring task force of an organization.

Compare Actual Performance Against the Established Targets

Strategic management is to select the best decision out of the set of decisions. Therefore, strategist should estimate future targets on the basis past and present performance the organization. Therefore, in this stage, comparison is essentially needed for the past, present and future performance of the organization.

Evaluate results and Take Action if Necessary

Evaluate results and take action if necessary is the last stage of the evaluating, monitoring and guided to the strategy to the CEO, managers and finally response from the low level employees of the organization. Top managers spent huge time for policy making and monitoring of the overall project of the organization. Strategy always leads to achieve even with the difficult external environment. This goal is to continually enhance an organization's competitive advantage.

LEVELS OF CONTROL

Organization performance is measured at four levels

levels are involved to control organizational structure. They are as follows:

Corporate level managers
Divisional level managers
Functional level managers
First level managers

Managers at the corporate level are most concerned with overall and abstract measures of organizational performance like profit, return on investment or total labor force turnover. The main aim is to choose performance standards. It measures overall corporate performance. Similarly, mangers at the other levels are most concerned with developing a set of standards to evaluate business or functional level performance. These measures should be closely tied to possible task force activities and accomplishment of the corporate objectives.

TYPES OF STRATEGIC CONTROL

There are six types of strategic control. They are as listed below:

- Premise control
- Implementation control
- Strategic surveillance
- Special alert control
- Market control
- Output control

Premise Control

Strategy is based on assumed or predicted conditions. These predictions or assumptions are planning premises. Company's strategy can be designed around these predicted conditions. Premise control can be designed to check systematically and continuously.

Whether premises set during the planning and implementation process are still valid or not valid. If a vital premise is no longer valid, therefore, then the strategy may have to be changed and premise can be recognized and revised for the better changes and acceptable.

Premises are primarily concerned with two factors are listed below:
Environmental factors
Industry factors

Environmental Factors

A company has little or no controllable other environmental factors. But these factors exercise considerable influence over the success of the strategy. Environmental factors like Inflation, technology, interest rates, regulation, demography and social changes etc. These factors are influenced to strategy formulating, implementation and control and monitoring of premises.

Industry Factors

Industry factors like competitors, suppliers, substitutes and barriers to entry. These are a few examples to affect the performance of industry. Industry factor differs from one industry to another industry. A company should aware of the factors that influence success for particular industry.

Premises are some major and some minor. Premises are often make about numerous environmental and industry variables, therefore, to attempt to track every premise may be must select premises and variables on the basis likely to change and would have a major impact on the company and its strategy.

The key premises should be identified during the planning process. The premises should be recorded and responsibly for monitoring, then should be assigned to the persons to departments who are qualified sources of information.

Implementation Control
The implementation control phase is an important phase of strategic management. It locates in the series of steps, programmmes, investments and moves undertaken over a period to implement to strategy. In this stage, special programmes are undertaken by company to implement

and control for accomplishment of objectives. A company function areas initiate several strategies that relate to mangers convert broad strategic plans into concrete actions and results for specific units and individuals for implementing strategy.

Implementation control can be designed to assess whether the overall strategy should be changed in light of unfolding events and results associated with incremental steps and actions. There are two basic factors involved in implementation control. They are listed below:

Monitoring strategic thrusts / projects

Milestone reviews

Monitoring Strategic Thrusts /projects

It involves implementation of strategies in companies that undertaking several new strategic projects or thrusts. These projects or thrusts provide a source of information to the manager. Strategic manager can obtain the information from the feedback. It helps to determine either the overall strategy can be progressed as planned or it needs to be adjusted to change.

There are two important approaches are useful in enacting implementation control. It focuses on monitoring strategic projects. They are as listed below:
The planning process of projects or thrusts.
Monitoring strategic projects or thrusts

Milestone Reviews
Mangers are attempted to identify critical milestone in organization. It will occur over the time period. Strategy can be implemented in a critical milestone like major resource allocations. In each critical case, it reviews and full-scale reassessment of the strategy and advisability of continuing or refocusing the direction of the organization or company.

Strategic Surveillance
Strategic surveillance can be designed to monitor a broad range of events inside and outside the company or organization. They are likely to threaten the course of the company's or organization's strategy. It should be

encouraged in the form of monitoring a source of information.

Special Alert Control

Another type of strategic controls is a special alert control. A special alert control can be needed to thoroughly and often rapidly reconsider the company's or organization basic strategy. It based on a sudden and unexpected event.

Market Control

It is an important objective of output control. It is helpful to strategist for analysis, monitoring the marketing performance of organization. Market control focus on the performance of one company to compare with another company in terms of stock market price and return on investment. These things help to appraise the financial performance of the company or organization.

Output Control

This is the last type of control system designs of the company or organization. Output control concentration on output like divisional goals, functional goals, individual goals which monitoring, evaluating and guided by the strategic mangers. Strategic manager aims to establish projects with execution of different types of control systems for measuring and improving efficiency of the organizational strategic objectives.

OPERATIONAL CONTROL SYSTEMS

Strategic control concerns with "steering" with company's future direction. Strategic control can be useful to top management in monitoring and steering the basic strategic direction of the company. Therefore, operating mangers also need appropriate control methods at all levels for strategy formulation and implementation and control operational system of an organization or company. The primary aim of the operating level can be allocated and use of the company's resources.

Operational control systems can guide, monitor and evaluate progress in current objectives of the company. Effective operational control systems must take into four steps. They are as below:
    Set standards of performance
    Measure actual performance

Identify deviations from standards

Initiate corrective action or adjustment

TYPES OF OPERATIONAL CONTROL SYSTEMS

There are three types of operational control systems. They are as listed below:

- Budgeting systems
- Scheduling
- Key success factors

Budgeting Systems

Budgeting systems provide for efficient resource allocation among the divisions /functions of the company. A budget involves to simply resource allocation plan, helps managers for coordination operations and facilitates managerial control.

Types of strategic Budgets

There are three types of Strategic budget are listed below:

- Revenue budgets
- Capital budgets
- Expenditure budgets

Revenue Budgets

Companies are prepared revenue budget to monitor their sources of revenue /income of the organization. The revenue budget has provided important information for the daily management of financial resources and key feedback as to whether for strategy is working. A revenue budget is particularly important as a tool for control of strategy implementation. It has provided an early warning system about the effectiveness of the company's strategy.

Capital Budgets

Capital budgets look for specific expenditures for plant, equipment, machinery, inventories and other capital items are needed during the budget period. Always Organization looks for strong sales. It can only to a strong growth of the organization. Capital is required for diversification /retrenchment of its current operations to generate additional resources. It carefully plans the acquisition and expenditure of funds for effective control. A company additional to prepare another two budgets as mention below:

Cash budget: It forecasts receipt and expenditure of the organization.

Balance sheet: it forecasts the status of assets, liabilities and net worth at the end of the budget period.

Expenditure Budgets

Expenditure budget aims to record all expenditure belongs to division /function of the organization. Expenditure budgets introduction is necessary to company to control and implementation of strategy in various operating units of the company. It can set standards to assess expenditure of the all divisions /functions of the organization. It can provide an effective communication link between top management and operating managers. It provides another warning system which alerting management of problems in the implementation of the company's strategy.

Scheduling

Scheduling is the key factor in the success of the strategy. It is simply a planning tool for allocating the use of a time-constrained resource or arranging the sequence of interdependent activities. Scheduling offers a mechanism with which to plan for, monitor and control these dependencies.

Key Success Factor

Key factors are very important to implementation of the project. Successful key factors are listed below:

Improved productivity

High employee morale

Improved product/service quality

Growth in market share

Completion of new facilities

Monitoring Performance and Evaluating

Organization carefully watches all goals, objectives that discharged by employees of the organization. A successful measure is a monitoring all activities of divisions /functions. It can be the best way reduced the errors and mistakes and brings very good productivity. Then we shall accomplishment of the objectives of the organization. Control can be needed all activities of the company.

STRATEGIC REWARD SYSTEM

Strategic reward system is also important to implement, control and monitoring the activities of the organization. Top-level executives want strategic reward in terms of

Praise

Recognition

Morale support

While in the case of middle level and low level management employees want strategic reward in terms of;

Piecework plans

Commission systems

Bonus plans

Profit sharing systems

Employee stock option systems

These benefits provide to employees to control and monitor the organizational activities.

www.ingramcontent.com/pod-product-compliance
Lightning Source LLC
Chambersburg PA
CBHW031423210526
45464CB00005B/2016